How Are You Feeling Today?

Seed
Learning

OK

great

angry

bored

excited

sick

sleepy

fantastic

How are you feeling today?

I'm OK.

How are you feeling today?

I'm angry.

How are you feeling today?

I'm excited.

How are you feeling today?

I'm bored.

How are you feeling today?

I'm fantastic!

Let's learn about Turkey.

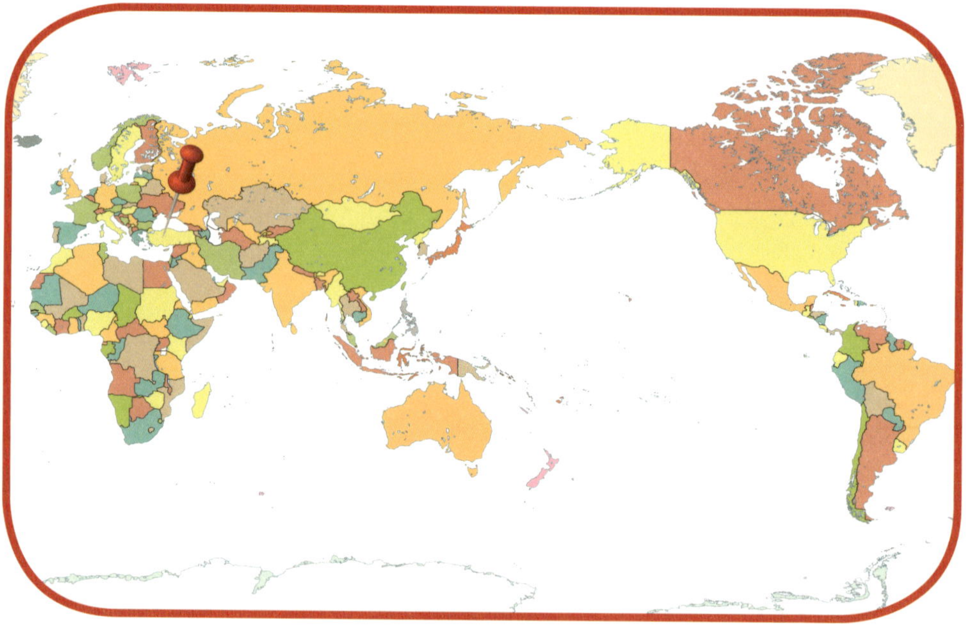

Flag of Turkey

Blue Mosque